The Fifty-Minute CAREER DISCOVERY Program—Revised

Elwood N. Chapman

A FIFTY-MINUTE™ SERIES BOOK

:50™

Viva Books Private Limited
New Delhi • Mumbai • Chennai • Kolkata • Hyderabad • Bangalore

First Indian Edition 2004

VIVA BOOKS PRIVATE LIMITED

- 4262/3 Ansari Road, Daryaganj, New Delhi 110 002
  E-mail: viva@vivagroupindia.net
- 215-216 New Apollo Estate, 2nd Floor, Mogra Lane, Andheri (E), Mumbai 400 069
  E-mail: vivamumbai@vivagroupindia.net
- Jamals Fazal Chambers, 26 Greams Road, Chennai 600 006
  E-mail: vivachennai@vivagroupindia.net
- B-103, Jindal Towers, 21/1A/3, Darga Road, Kolkata-700 017
  E-mail: vivakolkata@vivagroupindia.net
- 7 GF, Sovereign Park Apts., 56-58 K. R. Road, Basavanagudi, Bangalore 560 004
  E-mail: vivabangalore@vivagroupindia.net
- 101-102, First Floor, Mughal Marg Appartments, Narayanaguda Hyderbad
  E-mail: vivahyderbad@vivagroupindia.net

Published by arrangement with

Crisp Publications, Inc.
1200 Hamilton Court,
Menlo Park
CA 94025
USA

Credits:
Editor: Michael Crisp
Designer: Carol Harris
Typesetting: Interface Studio
Cover Design: Carol Harris

ISBN 81-7649-528-X

Published by Vinod Vasishtha for Viva Books Private Limited, 4262/3 Ansari Road, New Delhi 110 002. Printed and bound in India by Sanat Printers, Kundli - 131 028.

''How did I get here? Somebody pushed me. Somebody must have set me off in this direction and clusters of other hands must have touched themselves to the controls at various time, for I would not have picked this way for the world.''

Joseph Heller

ABOUT THIS BOOK

This Fifty-Minute CAREER DISCOVERY program (WRITE YOUR OWN CAREER SCRIPT) is not like most books. It stands out from others in an important way. It is not a book to read—it's a book to *use*. The unique "self-paced" format and the many exercises encourage the reader to get involved and try some new ideas immediately.

This publication will introduce the critical building blocks of how to conduct an effective career search. Using the simple but sound system presented can make dramatic changes in one's life and future happiness.

CAREER DISCOVERY (and other books listed on page 79) can be used effectively in a number of ways. Here are some posibilities.

—**Individual study.** Because the book is self-instructional, all that is needed is a quiet place, some time and a pencil. By completing the activities and exercises, most readers will come up with realistic career choices in about an hour.

—**Workshops and Seminars.** The book is effective in career exploration courses. Students can "work through" the system with class support as a "first" step to a more in-depth program under the guidance of a professional.

—**Resource for Courses With a Career Unit.** Many teachers like to add a career unit to their course content. The low cost of CAREER DISCOVERY makes it possible for students to own their own copy.

CAREER DISCOVERY is part of a series called BE TRUE TO YOUR FUTURE. Other books include a I GOT THE JOB! and PLAN B: PROTECTING YOUR CAREER FROM THE WINDS OF CHANGE.

CONTENTS

DARE TO DREAM

How can you be true to your future if you don't know what it holds? Good question! Although the future is unpredictable, everyone can have a direct influence on how things turn out. The most successful individuals understand the importance of having a plan which will help them accomplish their dreams. Unfortunately, a majority of individuals seem to exist on a day to day basis. To these people, life consists of ''marking time''.

Although planning for the future is always tentative, without a plan, there is less chance of a dream coming true. Thus it is important when planning your future to include some high expectations, even though they may appear slightly out of reach. If you do not set your goals high, you may miss out on some great life experiences.

This publication dares you to dream. Then, as a major step to fulfillment, you will be presented with a career discovery strategy that works. All you need is a pencil and some time.

Good luck!

PART I

TIE YOUR CAREER SEARCH TO A LIFE GOAL

START OUT THINKING BIG

A prime reason people find it difficult to discover the right career is because they do not link their efforts to a life goal. Without developing a ''bigger picture'', it is easy to drift like a space ship without a guidance system. A destination is never reached.

Isolating the right life goal for you is not easy or automatic. What is required is concentration and a road map. This book will provide the map if you furnish the concentration.

A good way to begin is to stop looking at college degrees, career possibilities, or job opportunities as ends in themselves. Rather, they should be viewed as vehicles to take you where you really want to go. At first, this may seem overwhelming, but all it really means is that you need to refocus your present thinking. You need to think beyond a degree, a career, or a job. You need to think bigger.

> When Brad first started searching for a career he followed a set pattern prescribed by a guidance specialist. The system was workable but Brad lost interest. He felt like he was trying to find a street address in a strange city without directions, thus there was little motivation to sustain his search. Some years later, after Brad identified a life goal for himself, he returned to a similar career search system with success.

One should avoid coming up with a life goal that is too nebulous to be of use. To be beneficial a goal should be sufficiently clear and strong to establish a set of priorities that provides both direction and enthusiasm.

Please do not get the idea that to be worthwhile your life goal must be highly altruistic or euphoric. Very few individuals will make a significant scientific discover, win a Nobel prize, or be voted most valuable player of a professional sports team. Your realistic life goal may be very practical. It could be:

- raising a happy family in a wholesome environment,
- building your dream home from scratch,
- improving personal health (longevity) for yourself and your family,
- having a career that makes other people happy,
- achieving recognition through creative efforts,
- creating an estate, or
- preparing for a carefree retirement.

LIFE GOALS DIFFER FROM OTHER GOALS

The ideal life goal will provide inspiration over a lifespan. It can be a daily "booster shot" to one's attitude. While a life goal might be gaining recognition from others through a significant achievement; more frequently it is something more personal. Those lucky enough to have a meaningful life goal seem to have more spirit, substance, and direction in their daily lives. And when a crisis occurs, they seem to handle it better than those without a life goal.

It is easy to confuse a life goal with other worthy aspirations. For example, earning a college degree is a significant accomplishment, however it is not normally a life goal. Buying a home is also a worthy objective, but unless there are some special circumstances (like designing and building it yourself) it is not, for most people, a life goal.

You may have thought of a career and life goal as one and the same. This is not always so. In the case of teaching, it might be said that teaching is a career but the life goal (the bigger concept) is a desire to help others learn. A life goal is usually expressed as something more personal and beyond the framework of a career. Often when one chooses a career as a life goal, something is missing. When the career ends, life may not have the meaning the person hoped to enjoy.

CAREER GOALS CAN BECOME LIFE GOALS

For some individuals a career goal can develop into a life goal. When this happens, it is a fortunate occurance.

> George, in his early years, became so involved in becoming a lawyer that he didn't pay any attention to life goals. His passion to become a successful lawyer was all that mattered. Fortunately, some years after he started his practice, George discovered that helping older people was something he really wanted to do. As a result, George changed his practice to specialize in estates and trusts. This allowed him to make a more significant contribution directly helping others. His early career choice eventually led him to his life goal.

Of course, it works both ways. Sometimes a life goal will lead an individual to the best career.

So which should come first?

The premise of this book is that as difficult as it may be to accomplish, the identification of a life goal should come first. This is because such a discovery can motivate an individual to make the best possible career search. People like George (in the situation above who knew early in life what he wanted to be) are in the minority. Most of us need some inspiration to help us complete a career search and job-finding campaign. Having a life goal will motivate us and make our career choice more valid.

BRINGING YOUR LIFE INTO FOCUS

Most people genuinely desire a life goal. They *want* something beyond a career or a job.

Seldom do life goals come easy. Most of us will ultimately succeed achieving a life goal if we stick with it, because life goals are within most of us. They are *there* if we can find a way to bring them to the surface. To help you do this, answer this question:

WHAT DO YOU REALLY WANT TO ACCOMPLISH THAT WILL GIVE YOU A SENSE OF LASTING FULFILLMENT?

Another approach is to project yourself into the future and imagine you are looking back on your life. Then ask yourself:

WHAT COULD I HAVE DONE THAT WOULD HAVE GIVEN MY LIFE MORE MEANING?

Because life goals are personal, you may or may not want to share the answers to the above questions with others. Often, however, an open discussion with an appropriate person may help bring your goal or goals into focus.

Although it may be ideal to think about life goals as always being worthy or contributing to humanity, this is not always the case. Some goals, such as accumulating personal wealth, or achieving great power are not altruistic. Yet these can be life goals, because they are highly motivating to some people over an extended period of time.

THE LIFE GOAL CHOICE IS YOURS ALONE

No other person can define a life goal for you or impose one on you. Your goal must come from within. In reality, it is not so much what your stated goal may be as much as the motivation it gives you to make the most of your life. Sadly, even though we only pass through this life once, many of us will never take the time to identify a life goal. Thus most of us drift, or plod. And find less fulfillment.

The following life goal profiles were developed to help you begin a process of isolation and clarification leading to your life goal. It does this by providing examples of how other people came up with life goals and how this discovery helped them select an appropriate career. As you proceed, remember that minds are like parachutes—they don't function until they are open.

LIFE GOAL PROFILES

Following are seven examples that illustrate the significant relationship between life goals and career choice. Please ☑ the three with which you most closely identify.

☐ More than anything Jake wants money. Having grown up lacking material goods, Jake sincerely wants financial security and an affluent lifestyle. So strong is his desire, that he intends to remain single until his goal is well on the way to reality. Although some of Jake's friends consider him to be narrow-minded and selfish, his goal motivated him to do a comprehensive career search, become a CPA, and accumulate more wealth than any of his old friends. Jake makes no apologies.

☐ Freda has two life goals. One is to travel; the other is to promote international understanding. Freda struggled over a long period of time to reach her goals. As a result, she was almost 40 when she became a travel agent. Thanks to ongoing courses, Freda was bilingual. During her travels, Freda works hard at being a "good will ambassador." Freda tells her friends: "Everything fell into place when I discovered something bigger to devote my life to. I wish I had concentrated on finding a good life goal sooner."

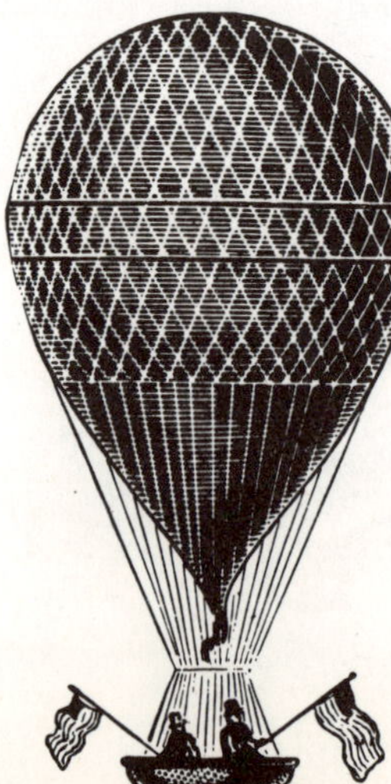

☐ Jennifer aborted two or three career search efforts and drifted from one job to another for ten years. Nothing came into focus. Then she met a special man and became a born again Christian. This provided her with the insight and motivation to find a career with meaning. Today Jennifer is married to her special man and is a happy, respected professional youth leader in a large midwestern church.

☐ When Mark and Julie ended their marriage, Julie's goal was to be a good parent and provider for their son Jimmy. With help from a college guidance center, she decided to find a career that allowed her to work at home. Computer programming was a perfect solution. Julie was able to find a job that had stability, good income, and allowed her to work at home so she could be with her son. It is a great career with future possibilities, all because Julie put Jimmy first.

☐ Raymond completed two years of college before "stopping out" to do a hitch in the Marine Corps. Following his discharge, he worked in construction as a laborer for three years. He never gave much thought to a career. Then he met Sue. For the first time in his life he wanted a future. By the time they became engaged, Raymond had decided he wanted to complete his college education and become an engineer.

LIFE GOAL PROFILES (Continued)

☐ Jose learned from an elementary school teacher that he had artistic talent. Later, even though he was encouraged to continue his education, Jose became a high school drop out. After moving from one unfulfilling job to another, he decided there was more to life. Then he met a Hispanic artist who made a good living through his art. Jose decided he could do as well and made the artist a role model. He returned to school and today Jose is a successful commercial artist and is frequently invited back to his old school as a speaker.

☐ After 25 years as a long-haul truck driver, Jack was forced to quit because of a back injury. For two years he lived off of his disability payments and showed little interest in the future. Then he and his wife were invited to take a trip in an R.V. by friends. The experience was so much fun that Jack and his wife came up with a life goal: to buy an R.V. and build a retirement plan around it! This motivated Jack to accept a job selling R.V.'s. He became so good at it, he now is part owner of a very successful R.V. dealership.

LIFE GOALS CAN CHANGE

Like career choices, or jobs, life goals are not frozen in cement. Although the vignettes in the life goal profiles demonstrated that powerful goals often surface, it does not mean one might not give way to another at a later date. Life goals need to be reviewed, maintained, restored, and sometimes replaced.

Before you start a career search, it is important to establish at least a tentative life goal. It need not fully satisfy you at this time, but at least it should assist you to find the best possible current career choice. Should you discover a more significant life goal once you have made a career choice, nothing has been lost. In many situations one career has a way of complimenting and supporting another.

On the following page is a diagram. Please complete it. The large star in the middle contains spaces for three life goals. Write in one, two or three.

Once you have recorded your goal or goals you have written the first page of your career script.

GIVE IT YOUR BEST SHOT

TIE CAREER ACTIVITIES TO LIFE GOALS

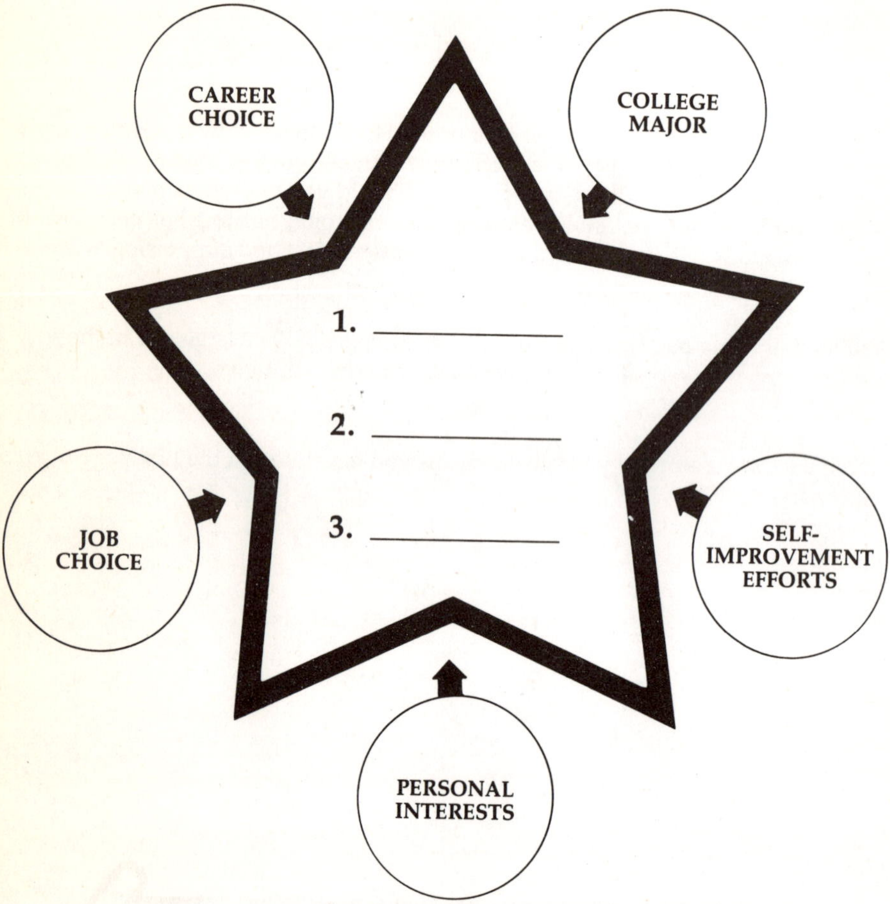

PART II

KNOWING YOURSELF

WHAT ROLES WILL YOU PLAY IN LIFE?

In a very real sense, you write your own script in life. This is because you have considerable freedom to select one career or job over another. You can also become the producer and director of your script. If you wish you can write yourself in as a star; or if you desire a less conspicuous role as a bit player. The choices are many and they are all yours. Exciting!

In the past it was normal for college students to declare a major related to a career; complete a prescribed curriculum of studies; find a job in that field; and often stick with it until retirement. One decision and that was it! Today it is far more common for people to change their majors, do several career searches, (and changes) in a lifetime. Some change careers because they did not make a wise choice initally; others because the one they selected has become obsolete or unsatisfactory; and still others want to match their changing values against a new career possibility.

A career search should not be confused with job-hunting. Finding the right career is an inward search. Finding the right job within a career is a totally different process.* A career search requires a demanding exploration which will direct you to selected academic or vocational training or education. In contrast, job-finding is an outward search. One makes an expedition into the world of work to find the best job available within a given career choice. Discovering and qualifying for a career can take years; getting the best job in a chosen area can, with luck, be accomplished in a few weeks. Job-hunting is, in effect, an appendage to a more complicated and extensive previous career search.

*For an excellent book on finding a job, order *I Got The Job!*

WHY A CAREER SEARCH WILL HELP YOU KNOW YOURSELF BETTER

When you look inwardly and search for a career choice you are also searching for your true identity. You are (perhaps without being aware of it) trying to define who you are, because the more you know about yourself, (traits, characteristics, differences) the better you can project yourself into a suitable career role.

Greg made an attempt at a career search before he dropped out of college and joined the Air Force. He made little progress. After four years, shortly before his discharge, he completed a successful search. The difference? Greg went through considerable introspection and ''growing up'' in the service. As a result, the second time around he knew himself better and knew what he really wanted. It was much easier for Greg to project himself into a comfortable career.

After her divorce, Macy went through an identity crisis. She became confused about her future and lost her confidence. It took help, but Macy came out of professional counseling knowing herself far better. Earlier, in trying to decide on a career she became frustrated and backed away. This time she followed a logical career search (similar to the one presented in this book) with confidence and found a career that was in harmony with the ''real'' Macy.

Greg and Macy demonstrate that the more you know about yourself the easier and more successful a career search should be. Of course, maturity cannot be forced, but you *can* take time to use certain psychological instruments to help you look closely at who you are and what you want to be. A professional guidance counselor (in your local community college for example), can administer certain testing instruments and help you project ahead to when you are a more "mature" person for career purposes. This is what they are trained to do.

As you engage in a search process (either with or without a professional counselor) keep in mind that nothing will work well unless you are honest with yourself. Only you know your values and only you know what will make you happy. It is also essential for you to acknowledge you are primarily responsible for your career script. It would be depressing to wind up at age sixty and realize you spent your working life producing the wrong movie. Do not let others assume the responsibility that belongs to you. Choosing a career is your decision and your opportunity. Only you can be true to your future.

> *"If one advances confidently in the direction of his dreams, and endeavors to live the life which he has imagined, he will meet with success unexpected in common hours."*
>
> *Henry David Thoreau*

WHAT VALUES WILL YOU FEATURE?

A value is a personal standard that you feel to be extremely important. For example, a career that allows you freedom on a daily basis may be more important to you than achieving status from peers. Thus you should consider a career that is less confining over one that provides high recognition but close supervision. Perhaps helping others (showing compassion for those less fortunate) is more important for you than money. If so you probably would prefer a career that provides opportunities to counsel and help others even though the pay may be modest.

Think of values as precious jewels that can adorn and enhance your life. Your values make you unique. When you are true to them, you are in harmony with yourself. Values should be worn quietly and with style.

Values need to be given high priority because when they are compatible with a career choice, you are getting a signal that you will be happy and successful in that particular career. This means that (as far as possible) you should recognize your primary values before undertaking a career search. Easy to say but sometimes difficult to accomplish.

Doing the exercise on the following page will help you clarify your values. The idea is to get you to identify your *three most basic values.* These will be important to take with you during your career search.

GET IN TOUCH WITH YOUR VALUES

This exercise is designed to help you identify your primary values. Please place a ☑ in the appropriate square. Once you have finished, circle three from the "very important" column that you intend to keep in mind during your search.

Values	*Very Important*	*Somewhat Important*	*Not Important*
Being free.	☐	☐	☐
Helping others.	☐	☐	☐
Making money.	☐	☐	☐
Working outdoors.	☐	☐	☐
Having a steady job.	☐	☐	☐
Having people respect me.	☐	☐	☐
Having my kind of lifestyle.	☐	☐	☐
Opportunity to learn.	☐	☐	☐
Working regular hours.	☐	☐	☐
Achieving my creative potential.	☐	☐	☐
Experiencing career fulfillment.	☐	☐	☐
Working with people I like.	☐	☐	☐
Doing technical work.	☐	☐	☐
Exhibiting leadership.	☐	☐	☐
Putting my personal life ahead of my job.	☐	☐	☐
Living where I want to live.	☐	☐	☐

My three "most important" values are:

1. ______________________________

2. ______________________________

3. ______________________________

If you do not remain true to those values you checked "very important" you may make the wrong career choice.

CASE #1

CASE #1

Most individuals eventually discover there are tradeoffs between career and lifestyle. Few find careers which blend perfectly. Most must learn to balance both worlds—this usually means compromising.

A PROBLEM FOR JOYCE

Joyce is an outstanding organizer. For example, in high school, she organized a campaign that won her the position of student body president. She loves to manage and motivate people. Leading others is a thrill. Joyce has decided to become a Business Administration major and try her luck as a manager.

There is only one problem with her major. Joyce also loves animals. So much, in fact, that she has seriously considered becoming a veterinarian. In addition, she feels more comfortable in a rural setting. She seems happier when she is on her parent's farm with the horses, dogs and other animals.

The conflict is obvious. Joyce has always pictured herself living in a country setting surrounded by animals. A job as an executive would probably mean living in a big city and likely moving from time to time. She has heard over and over that to become an executive she must be willing to change organizations when required, work long hours and put her work over her personal lifestyle.

Joyce is a college sophomore so there is plenty of time for her to switch majors.

What would you suggest for Joyce? Should she continue to seek a career in business or should she explore becoming a veterinarian? Can she have a successful career as an executive and still have the lifestyle she wants? Write your opinion in the spaces below and compare with that of the author on page 73.

____

____

____

____

YOUR INTERESTS NEED TO BE CONSIDERED

An interest is a curiosity you possess about certain aspects of your environment. Although you may have various degrees of interest in many things; there are probably a few areas where your interest is more intense and lasting. These high level interests will influence your career choice. A keen interest in people has led many to a successful career as a teacher or counselor; a deep interest in the wilderness has produced some professional foresters; an early and consistent interest in reading and books has developed some outstanding librarians.

The special interests you can identify should be given consideration (along with your values) when making a career choice. There are some excellent Interest Inventories (such as the Strong-Campbell or Kuder DD) that will help you pinpoint and rank your interests. These inventories are based on years of research and have proven to help a person select a career where he or she is happy. You are encouraged to take an interest inventory. These are available at almost all college guidance centers for a very modest price. You should then have it interpreted for you by a guidance professional at the location where you are tested. What you learn could be extremely rewarding.

For the purposes of this investigation, please list what you believe to be your top three primary and permanent interests. Do this now.

1.

2.

3.

P.S. It will be interesting for you to compare what you listed above with the results of an interest inventory (if you take one). You might be surprised.

GIVE ANY APTITUDES YOU POSSESS TOP BILLING!

Aptitude implies a natural inclination for a particular kind of work. Translated, this means an ability to quickly master a particular skill.

> As a child, Gus had fun "tinkering" with his toys. He helped his dad do automobile repairs before he had his drivers license. Later Gus found math to be his favorite course. When he did a career search Gus looked for opportunities to capitalize on his special aptitude. No one was surprised when he became a mechanical engineer.

> Gretchen learned to operate a personal computer far ahead of her classmates. She not only took to the keyboard and word processor quickly, Gretchen also enjoyed words, sentence construction, and became excellent at spelling. When it came time to select a career, she was quickly drawn to the office occupation area.

Various aptitude tests are available in most career centers. The mechanical and clerical instruments are the most popular. Should you score high in an aptitude test, it suggests you will have a high probability of success in those careers where that aptitude is important.

If you feel you have a high clerical, mechanical or other aptitude place a ☑ in the appropriate square, then arrange to take a test to confirm your feelings.

☐ Mechanical aptitude

☐ Clerical aptitude

☐ Other: ____________________

SPOTLIGHT YOUR SPECIAL TALENTS

Talents are often confused with aptitudes. We define a talent as a superior, often natural, ability. Talents cover a wide variety of fields. Talent is easy to identify in areas such as the arts or athletics. When people refer to the talent of another, they often use the word "gift". Examples of special talents include outstanding singing or speaking voice, an ability to act, sculpt, play a musical instrument, draw, paint, write, run, throw, kick, jump, hit a ball, swim, etc.

When Marise first started to ice skate she sensed she had more talent than her friends. Recognizing this early, Marise was motivated to devote hours to practice her skills. Through the support of teachers and family members, she became a professional skater and skating instructor.

Geraldine had been in the church choir for only two practice sessions when the leader complimented her on her clear, unusual voice. Ten years (and many voice lessons later) Geraldine became a popular "rock" singer.

Some people tie a lifelong career to a single talent. A few succeed, but many fail and eventually suffer burnout or disappointment. To guard against this, these individuals might consider different ways to use their special talent in *several* career possibilities.

List any special talents you have below.

1. ______________________________

2. ______________________________

3. ______________________________

YOU CAN'T WRITE A SUCCESSFUL CAREER SCRIPT WITHOUT KNOWING YOUR VALUES, INTERESTS, APTITUDES, TALENTS AND ABILITIES.

BE ALL THAT YOU CAN BE!

In choosing a career, both physical and mental ability should be considered. Top high school and college athletes (in concert with their coaches) need to assess their physical abilities as a prelude to a possible career in professional sports. Other students (through grades and competitive tests) receive signals on how they rank in mental ability compared to others.

The expression "you can be anything you want to be" is not true. For example, only a tiny fraction of athletes are good enough to become a professional basketball player. Not everyone can pass a bar exam regardless of how much formal education they receive, or how many times they take the examination. It is important to be realistic about our ability to succeed in certain careers.

On the other hand, some people do not live up to their potential. We refer to these individuals as underachievers.

> Casey neglected to complete work he was easily capable of doing while in high school. As a result he spent ten years in a menial job. Casey has since returned to school (evening program) and is now a successful small business owner.

Some of us try to reach beyond our capabilities and create unnecessary pressures on ourselves. We refer to these individuals as overachievers.

> Barbara decided in high school to become a research chemist and spent the next eight years trying to qualify without success. Her extreme efforts almost resulted in a nervous breakdown. Thanks to a sensitive counselor, Barbara was channeled into a less demanding career where she uses chemistry and enjoys a high degree of satisfaction.

Everyone needs to find a career that challenges them physically or mentally but, at the same time, falls within their "range"

Name a career beyond your physical or mental ability: ____________________

Name a career beneath your physical or mental ability: ____________________

CASE #2

CASE #2

Finding a career is one thing—knowing you can qualify educationally is something else. It is vital you select a career that is within your academic range.

JAKE'S DILEMMA

Jake is totally discouraged because of a conversation he had yesterday with his engineering professor. The instructor called Jake into his office after giving him a failing grade on the midterm examination and said: ''Jake, I'm afraid you may be on the wrong educational track. Engineering is a tough discipline and to make it, you must be academically sound in mathematics. If you stay in class, you will need to arrange for tutorial help. My feeling, however, is that you should drop out now, before you have too much invested and move into something less demanding.''

Jack is 28 years old and has six years of military training behind him. His years in the Navy convinced him he had excellent mechanical aptitudes. He proved he can repair almost anything. This was what made him elect to choose engineering as a degree choice. Jake's aptitude may be more in engineering application than theory. Some of his friends, for example, have encouraged him to change from electrical engineering to civil engineering.

Yesterday Jake met with his academic counselor who made three suggestions. First, Jake should be honest with himself. In addition to the F in the engineering midterm, Jake is doing poorly in chemistry. Second, Jake should investigate alternative academic courses. Third, if Jake is determined to become an electrical engineer, he should accept tutoring plus an additional year in college for basic remedial work in order to make the transition to a full engineering program.

Will Jake eventually become a degreed engineer? Write your opinion in the spaces below and compare with that of the author on page 73.

____

____

____

YOUR WORKING ENVIRONMENT

Your values, interests, aptitudes, talents, and physical/mental abilities are extremely important. The environment under which you must perform also deserves consideration. Would you be happy working 40 hours of shift work each week in a hospital? How about being confined to a science laboratory? Would you be comfortable wearing a uniform each day in a military environment?

> Angie became so involved becoming an outstanding computer analyst and advanced programmer that she neglected to think ahead about *where* she could start her career and under what conditions. Upon graduation, the only place where her abilities could be challenged was a computer center in an urban area. Result? A one hour commute, crowded office and a pace she did not anticipate. After two years, Angie accepted a less challenging job to get the kind of slower paced work environment she wanted.

In choosing a career, it is important to consider the following factors:

(1) The physical environment (i.e. type of office, location, parking, and the amount of freedom provided).

(2) People associations. Must you work as a team? Will you be with people you enjoy? Would you prefer to work alone?

(3) What about hours of employment? Will the environment be detrimental to your lifestyle and life goals?

Please list your ideal working environment preferences below:

____

____

Please list any working environments you would refuse to accept:

____

____

THE HAPPINESS FACTOR

Many people believe that if an individual can find a career (or careers) that makes him or her happy, everything else will take care of itself. The rationale goes like this: If you are happy you will automatically do a better job and this will eventually give you the recognition, money, power, personal satisfaction, and anything else you might want. In short, just find a career that will make you happy and you have it made.

The statement, like so many generalizations, does contain at least a kernel of truth. If you find a career that will make you happy, your chances of success are much improved. But happiness is a relative thing. Your career choices should be involving, in harmony with your personal values, and contribute to a purposeful and happy life. They will probably not lead you into a state of euphoria. In short, you may have to be satisfied with something less than pure happiness. An individual who achieves 80 percent job satisfaction is doing exceptionally well.

Generally speaking, finding a career that will make you happy is a matter of matching and balancing your values, abilities, interests, aptitudes, talents and feelings about your work environment with a particular career. The matter of compensation also deserves consideration. Many people might be happiest in careers such as free-lance writing, doing research in tropical flowers, hot air ballooning, or other exotic choices, but these careers might not produce enough income. Sometimes, in order to be true to your long-term future, compromises must be made during the early years of work. This is why it is essential to balance the various factors (values, interests, etc.) discussed in the previous pages.

Congratulations, you have completed Part II. We hope that you now know yourself somewhat better than when you started this section.

In Part III, you will learn how to conduct an effective career discovery search.

PART III

CONDUCTING YOUR SEARCH

CAREER GUIDANCE SPECIALISTS FEEL STRONGLY THAT A CAREER SEARCH IS THE BEST INVESTMENT IN TIME A PERSON CAN MAKE. WHEN YOU THINK ABOUT IT—THEY ARE PROBABLY RIGHT!

CASE #3

CASE #3

This case will help you understand some of the diverse elements involved in a successful career search.

WILL JOE FIND THE RIGHT CAREER?

After six weeks at a major university, Joe, a freshman, feels lost and frustrated. Despite working hard, Joe is not sure he is on the right educational track. What if he is taking courses that will lead him to the wrong career?

Although pressed for time, yesterday Joe stopped by the campus career center. He was pleased to find a counselor sincerely interested in helping him. After spending forty minutes talking with the counselor, Joe decided he would do the following before the end of the term.

1. Spend time in the career center looking through materials to see if he could find several realistic career possibilities.

2. Take an interest inventory and have the counselor interpret it for him.

3. Solicit opinions about possible careers from close friends and relatives.

4. Be *totally* honest about what he wants and what he is willing to do to achieve success.

5. Return to the counselor before making any major changes.

If Joe does everything listed, what chance do you feel he has of finding the right career? Place a check in the appropriate square.

EXCELLENT ☐ GOOD ☐ POOR ☐

Please turn to page 73 to compare your answer with that of the author.

LONG VS SHORT CAREER SEARCH

When it comes to finding the best career, three options are available. First, you can simply rely on your intuition and search accordingly. Second, you can do a brief, organized search on your own using this publication as a guide. Finally, you can conduct an extended, in-depth search (often in a class setting) under the guidance of an expert.

If you elect to follow your intuition (option 1) the probability of finding the "best" career is low. You might luck out, but most experts recommend against it. Spending a lifetime in the wrong career is a severe price to pay.

SHORT SEARCH

The advantage of a dedicated short search (as prescribed in this book) is that it can produce an immediate career direction using a tested procedure. True, it may not be as foolproof as a long search, but it is far better than simply relying on your own methods. A "short search" should not be considered a "quick fix." Reading this book may take only about one hour, but the concept has been tested and the results have a reasonable level of reliability. The process is logical, and the step-by-step system has value. Best of all, you can take the results from this book to career guidance specialists for additional support. We recommend this for serious career searches. This book is an important first step toward an in-depth search. So, no matter how you look at it, you have everything to gain and nothing to lose from completing the system in this book. Chances are good that you will find quality career choice options that relate to your life goal. Many readers will feel so good about it that they will begin being true to their future. We hope you find yourself in this group.

LONG SEARCH

For those with time and dedication, an in-depth search is highly recommended. Finding the best career *is* a complex undertaking but something that can affect how happy your life will be. It should be worth whatever time is required to make the best possible career choice.

Where can you start your serious search? Almost all colleges have a 1 or 2 unit career exploration program under the direction of a career professional. These courses last a full term (normally one or two hours per week). Most will involve taking a series of testing instruments (interest inventories, aptitude tests, personality profiles, etc.). A big advantage in enrolling in such a program is that you receive the psychological support of a guidance expert and can interact with others who are also looking for a career. Those who complete a program not only can end up with one or more exciting career choices, but also benefit from the search itself. Along the way, a person should get to know himself or herself much better.

A long search can also be accomplished on an individual basis under the guidance of a professional. This is often accomplished through the use of a short program which is supplemented with results from various testing instruments, individual counseling, and access to a career center. A career center can provide a wide variety of aids, including some recent sophisticated computerized programs.

Despite all of the help available, it is estimated that only 3% of college students take advantage of career programs. Why this figure is so low is a mystery.

BENEFITS FROM COMPLETING A CAREER SEARCH

Place a check in those squares where the statement has high credibility for you.

FINDING YOUR BEST CAREER CHOICE CAN:

- ☐ Help you achieve a ''life goal''
- ☐ Reduce the frustration that accompanies not knowing what to do with your life.
- ☐ Help you make the best use of your talents, aptitudes, and abilities.
- ☐ Motivate you to take advantage of available learning opportunities.
- ☐ Ultimately increase your income.
- ☐ Help you better understand ''who you are''
- ☐ Enhance your lifestyle.
- ☐ Cause you to have more confidence and feel better about yourself.

Are you teaming up with another person in making your search? Testing indicates that the team approach sometimes works well providing that (1) both individuals realize that they are special individuals and therefore have different career needs; (2) they do much of their research independently even though they may be together much of the time; and (3) they are both self-motivated so that if one becomes discouraged and stops, the other one does not automatically follow.

GETTING ON THE RIGHT TRACK

A railroad system has tracks leading in many directions. Each track leads to different stations. Obviously, if you don't get on the right track to start with, you cannot get to the right station without being re-routed.

The same is true in a career search. The most important thing you can do is to get on the right track as soon as possible so that you will wind up at the career station you want. This is especially true when selecting a college major. If you don't choose a major that will lead you to the right careers, (a few years later), you have taken the wrong train.

So what is the answer?

One answer is to identify a few specific career possibilities early and then try to fit them into certain career areas. If enough choices "fit", then you are in a position to select the right track to get there. THIS IS THE SYSTEM USED IN THIS PUBLICATION.

On the following page you are encouraged to list twenty (20) career possibilities for yourself. This may sound like a lot, but it takes that many to make the system work. Do not worry. You will be given all the help required to make your selections. As you do this, keep these two advantages in mind: (1) By stretching your list to twenty possibilities you may discover a career or career area you have neglected in your past thinking. (2) A base of twenty possibilities (you are encouraged to list more) makes the system logical and operative.

This all means that you should be able to find more than one station (specific career) on any track (general career area) you choose to follow. This will give you some significant signals you would not otherwise receive—signals that can reassure you that your search is going in the right direction.

PLEASE TRUST THE SYSTEM AND FOLLOW THE RULES ON THE NEXT PAGE.

TWENTY SPECIFIC CAREER POSSIBILITIES

You have been evaluating career possibilities since you were a child. Some of those which appealed at one time may be more reliable than you think. Reach into your memory and list career possibilities which have potential for you. When you have done this, turn the page and you will receive assistance on how to expand the list to a minimum of twenty.

Code Numbers

1.
2.
3.
4.
5.
6.
7.
8.
9.
10.
11.
12.
13.
14.
15.
16.
17.
18.
19.
20.

When you have twenty specific career possibilities listed above, please turn to page 41.

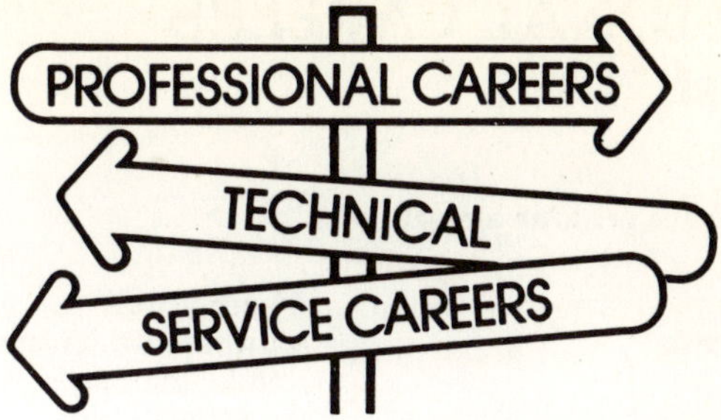

To help you find additional career possibilities, more than 200 popular career titles have been listed on the following three pages.* To make your decisions easier, they have been arbitrarily divided into three categories as described below. Please follow directions until you have twenty serious career prospects listed on page 36.

Professional careers almost always require a college degree. Is your mind geared toward the academic world? Do you enjoy learning? Do you have the self-discipline to complete a university program? Do you have your mind *set* on a four-year degree or beyond? If so, page 38 may contain career ideas that will help you complete your prospect list on page 36. Select only those that have high interest. If you do not find enough to complete your prospect list, investigate the categories below.

Technical careers are also professional in nature but do not always require a college education. Two years of college or completion of a technical college program is often sufficient. Mechanical and building careers are found in this category. If you are technically or mechanically inclined, turn to page 39 and give the careers listed careful consideration. If possible, select enough to build your prospect list to twenty. Also, explore the service category below.

Service careers often require a college degree, but not always. These careers offer great opportunity for those who like to work with people. Do you have a desire to serve others? Are people-oriented careers attractive to you? This is an excellent category for highly talented and educated people, but if you do not plan to graduate from a four-year college or university and technical careers have no appeal for you, this category may be your best bet. Please turn to page 40 and attempt to select enough careers from those listed to complete your prospect list on page 36.

(NOTE: Many of the careers listed in one of the above categories could be appropriate for another category. It is of no concern, the idea is to find twenty prospects.)

*For an expanded list see the Dictionary of Occupational Titles (DOT) at any library or career center. The DOT is published by the Employment & Training Division of the U.S. Department of Labor.

PROFESSIONAL CAREERS (Partial list)

Circle those that have genuine appeal.

Interpreter 4, 5, 1
Electrical Engineer 6
Dental Hygienist 8
Architect 5, 6
Chemical Engineer 6
Industrial Engineer 6
Aerospace Engineer 6
Home Economist 1, 5, 8
Industrial Designer 5, 6
Clergy 5
Zoologist 9
Journalist 5, 14
Dietician 8
Sanitarian 6
Meteorologist 9, 14
Librarian 5
Registered Nurse 8
Entomologist 9
Oceanographer 9, 14
Mathematician 6, 9, 1
Botanist 9
Lawyer 1, 2, 14
Optometrist 8
Statistician 4, 1, 14
FBI Agent 4
Chiropractor 8
Mechanical Engineer 6
Purchasing Agent 1
Physical Therapist 8
Public Administrator 4
Chemist 9
Sociologist 9, 5, 1
Author 5, 14
Machine Designer 6
Nuclear Scientist 9
Anthropologist 9, 5

Pharmacist 8
Business Administrator 1
Marketing Specialist 3
Forester 10
Actuary 1
Economist 9, 11
Military Officer 11
Teacher 5
Small Business Owner 13
Accountant 1
Banker 1
Psychiatrist 8
Landscape Architect 5, 10
Professional Counselor 5
Physician 8
Youth Leader 5
Dentist 8
Computer Analyst 2
Veterinarian 8
Psychologist 5, 8
Social Worker 4
Civil Engineer 6
Astronomer 9, 14
Computer Programmer 2
Geologist 9
Newscaster 5
Editor 5, 14
Advertising Manager 3, 5
Movie Producer 14, 5
Graphic Artist 5
Laser Specialist 9
Sales Manager 3
Communications Engineer 6
Human Resource Director 1
Certified Public Account 1

Other professional careers:

____________________ ____________________

____________________ ____________________

Add any career possibilities you circled above to those on page 36. Include code numbers.

TECHNICAL CAREERS (Partial list)

Circle those that have genuine appeal.

Surveyor 6, 7, 15
Carpenter 7
Draftsperson 7, 5
Airconditioning Technician 7
Painter - Paperhanger 7
Engineering Technician 7
Railroad Career 15
Automobile Body Repairperson 7
Automobile Mechanic 7
Bricklayer - Stonemason 7
Electronic Technician 7
Broadcasting Technician 7
Television, Radio Repairperson 7
Appliance Repairperson 7
Watch Repairperson 7
Machinist 7
Tool and Die Maker 7
Dental Technician 8
Molder - Coremaker 7
Factory Trainee 7
Medical Technician 8
Pilot 15, 14
Computer Technician 7
Laboratory Technician 8, 7
Airplane Mechanic 7
Diesel Mechanic 7
Millwright 7
Maintenance Electrician 7
U.S. Marines 11
U.S. Army 11
U.S. Air Force 11
U.S. Navy 11
Coast Guard 11
Maintenance Mechanic 7
Firefighter 4
Tilesetter 7
Plasterer 7
Plumber 7
Electrician 7
Business Machines Repairperson 7
Lithographer 5, 7
Forestry Aide 10
Cement Mason 7
Builder 13
Computer Repairperson 7
X-Ray Technician 8
Contractor 13
Barge Operator 14

Additional technical careers:

____________________ ____________________

____________________ ____________________

____________________ ____________________

Turn to page 36 and list those careers you circled above. Include code numbers. If you added a career to the list, be sure to include it.

SERVICE CAREERS (Partial list)

Circle those that have genuine appeal.

Fashion Designer 14, 5
Actor, Actress 14, 5
Truck, Bus Driver 15
Singer, Dancer, Model 5, 14
Mortician 14
Musician 5
Police Officer 4
Artist 5
Florist 5, 13
Travel Agent 13, 15
Professional Athlete 14
Retail Salesperson 3
Interior Designer 5
Decorator 5
Photographer 5, 13
Telephone Operator 1
Bank Teller 1
News Commentator 5, 14
Traffic Manager 7
Medical Lab Assistant 8
Cosmetologist 5
Automobile Salesperson 3
Guard 15
Restaurant Operator 13
Franchise Owner 13
Para-Medic 8
Museum Guide 14
Insurance Salesperson 3
Supermarket Trainee 15
Professional Salesperson 3
Chef, Cook, Baker 12
Restaurant Manager 12, 13
Waiter/Waitress 12
Bartender 12
Hostess 12
Postal Employee 4
Store Manager Trainee 1
Fashion Salesperson 3
Nurses Aide 8
Flight Attendant 14
Dental Assistant 8
Hotel Career 12
Clerk - Typist 2
Secretary 2
Computer Operator 2
Word Processor 2
Office Manager 2
Practical Nurse 8
Bookkeeper 2, 1
Stock Broker 3
Firefighter 4
Real Estate Salesperson 3
Disk Jockey 14
Hairstylist 5

Other service careers:

______________________ ______________________

______________________ ______________________

______________________ ______________________

Return to page 36 and list those careers you circled above. Include code numbers. If you added a career be sure to list it.

CAREER BOXES: YOUR SEARCH EXPANDS

By listing a minimum of twenty specific career possibilities on page 36 you have created a base from which you can more rationally determine which career track to take. The system works like this.

Specific careers usually come in clusters. For example, there are many kinds of medical doctors or nurses. These are small clusters. But it is possible to place all medical careers (hundreds) into one big cluster. When an individual shows interest in more than one career that falls within a cluster, this intensifies the interest and is a signal that this individual may be on the right career track.

> Nick independently selected four specific careers that wound up in a single cluster. This made Nick feel great because it was, in a sense, a discovery to realize all were related. Without knowing it, he was leaning in the direction of one career track over the others available.

You will find 15 Career Boxes (clusters) on the following pages. The idea is to assign your twenty specific career choices into the appropriate boxes. This will help you discover which directions you are headed in. The system employed is one of self-discovery.

The process is easy. If a career has a code number (from pages 38, 39, and 40) it should be listed in the box with the same number. In some cases, a specific career may have more than one code number. If so, it should be written in all of the boxes indicated.

If you prefer not to use the code numbers, or you list careers not found on pages 38, 39, or 40, thumb through the career boxes and assign the career to the box you feel is most appropriate. If you do not find a suitable box for a specific career, place it in box 15.

When each career has been written into the most appropriate box, please turn to page 57.

Career Box #1

GENERAL BUSINESS

(Management, production, warehousing, transportation. Does not include office occupations, sales and marketing, or owning your own business.)

THINK MANAGERIAL AND THE SUPERVISION OF OTHERS. This is the largest of all occupational areas. The work environment is highly competitive. Chances are good you would work for a large organization. Most Business majors fall into this category.

Specific Careers →
1.
2.
3.
4.
5.
6.
7.
8.
9.
10.

WILL THIS OCCUPATIONAL AREA;

	Yes	**No**
Measurably help you reach your life goals?	☐	☐
Be compatible with your values?	☐	☐
Capitalize on your special interests?	☐	☐
Challenge your mental abilities?	☐	☐
Take advantage of any aptitudes you were able to identify?	☐	☐
Make use of any special talents you may possess?	☐	☐
Provide the working environment you want?	☐	☐

Career Box #2

OFFICE OCCUPATIONS

(Accounting, secretarial, word processing, office managers, etc.)

THINK OFFICE AUTOMATION. Most employees in this area have basic computer competence and above average English and computational skills. Most jobs are performed within office environments in large cities. Commuting is normal.

Specific Careers →

1.
2.
3.
4.
5.
6.
7.
8.
9.
10.

WILL THIS OCCUPATIONAL AREA;

	Yes	No
Measurably help you reach your life goals?	☐	☐
Be compatible with your values?	☐	☐
Capitalize on your special interests?	☐	☐
Challenge your mental abilities?	☐	☐
Take advantage of any aptitudes you were able to identify?	☐	☐
Make use of any special talents you may possess?	☐	☐
Provide the working environment you want?	☐	☐

Career Box #3

SALES/MARKETING OCCUPATIONS
(Marketing specialists, sales representative for manufacturers, stock brokers and Real Estate professionals, retail sales people etc.)

THINK INTERACTING WITH OTHERS. Individuals in this area are normally out-going and enjoy people. They are also competitive and like daily challenges. They value freedom of movement and don't mind taking risks. Most enjoy the fast lane and are open to job changes.

Specific Careers ⟶ 1.

2.

3.

4.

5.

6.

7.

8.

9.

10.

WILL THIS OCCUPATIONAL AREA;

	Yes	No
Measurably help you reach your life goals?	☐	☐
Be compatible with your values?	☐	☐
Capitalize on your special interests?	☐	☐
Challenge your mental abilities?	☐	☐
Take advantage of any aptitudes you were able to identify?	☐	☐
Make use of any special talents you may possess?	☐	☐
Provide the working environment you want?	☐	☐

Career Box #4

GOVERNMENT AND SOCIAL SERVICE

(Police force, firefighter, postal employees, welfare counselor, probation officer, unemployment counselor, border patrol, etc.)

THINK CITY, COUNTY, STATE, AND FEDERAL AGENCY. This is an extremely large, diverse, and bureaucratic employment area. Although working environments are highly structured, opportunities are many. Job security and early retirement possibilities exist.

Specific Careers →
1.
2.
3.
4.
5.
6.
7.
8.
9.
10.

WILL THIS OCCUPATIONAL AREA;

	Yes	No
Measurably help you reach your life goals?	☐	☐
Be compatible with your values?	☐	☐
Capitalize on your special interests?	☐	☐
Challenge your mental abilities?	☐	☐
Take advantage of any aptitudes you were able to identify?	☐	☐
Make use of any special talents you may possess?	☐	☐
Provide the working environment you want?	☐	☐

Career Box #5

CREATIVE, EDUCATIONAL, RELIGIOUS

(Educators, teachers, ministers, entertainers, publishers, newscasters, youth leaders, etc.)

THINK VERBAL COMMUNICATIONS. This is generally a high visibility career area where individuals are creative and expressive. Most are leaders and like the feeling of being "in charge". Normal working hours are less important than the freedom to be creative.

Specific Careers → 1.

2.

3.

4.

5.

6.

7.

8.

9.

10.

WILL THIS OCCUPATIONAL AREA;

	Yes	No
Measurably help you reach your life goals?	☐	☐
Be compatible with your values?	☐	☐
Capitalize on your special interests?	☐	☐
Challenge your mental abilities?	☐	☐
Take advantage of any aptitudes you were able to identify?	☐	☐
Make use of any special talents you may possess?	☐	☐
Provide the working environment you want?	☐	☐

Career Box #6

HIGH TECH/ENGINEERS

(Computer science professionals, scientists, designers, engineers of many kinds, and the technicians that back them up.)

THINK MODERN TECHNOLOGY. This is a difficult occupational area to define but it helps to think of those who design, build, and maintain the complex technology around us. Often the job is in a laboratory environment. High level skills are normally required. Advanced academic degrees are common.

Specific Careers → 1.

2.

3.

4.

5.

6.

7.

8.

9.

10.

WILL THIS OCCUPATIONAL AREA;

	Yes	No
Measurably help you reach your life goals?	☐	☐
Be compatible with your values?	☐	☐
Capitalize on your special interests?	☐	☐
Challenge your mental abilities?	☐	☐
Take advantage of any aptitudes you were able to identify?	☐	☐
Make use of any special talents you may possess?	☐	☐
Provide the working environment you want?	☐	☐

Career Box #7

TRADES/CRAFTS

(Benchwork occupations, building trades, heavy-equipment operators, contractors, printing and textile occupations, etc.)

THINK BLUEPRINTS AND WORKING WITH YOUR HANDS. Most who select this area have a high mechanical aptitude. They like to see what they build. Many enjoy outdoor work. A sizable percentage work for themselves.

Specific Careers →

1.
2.
3.
4.
5.
6.
7.
8.
9.
10.

WILL THIS OCCUPATIONAL AREA;

	Yes	**No**
Measurably help you reach your life goals?	☐	☐
Be compatible with your values?	☐	☐
Capitalize on your special interests?	☐	☐
Challenge your mental abilities?	☐	☐
Take advantage of any aptitudes you were able to identify?	☐	☐
Make use of any special talents you may possess?	☐	☐
Provide the working environment you want?	☐	☐

Career Box #8

HEALTH SERVICES

(Doctors, dentists, veterinarians, nurses, paramedics, medical lab assistants, etc.)

THINK WHITE UNIFORMS/HOSPITALS/DENTAL OFFICES/CLINICS. The work environment of health services is easy to define. Most have a compassion for others and are willing to work odd-hours. Careers include everything from the physician with years of specialized training to a medical clerk just out of high school.

Specific Careers →
1.
2.
3.
4.
5.
6.
7.
8.
9.
10.

WILL THIS OCCUPATIONAL AREA;

	Yes	No
Measurably help you reach your life goals?	☐	☐
Be compatible with your values?	☐	☐
Capitalize on your special interests?	☐	☐
Challenge your mental abilities?	☐	☐
Take advantage of any aptitudes you were able to identify?	☐	☐
Make use of any special talents you may possess?	☐	☐
Provide the working environment you want?	☐	☐

Career Box #9

EARTH, PHYSICAL & BEHAVIORAL SCIENCES
(Biologist, zoologist, chemist, geologist, and other physical scientists; anthropologist, sociologist, political scientists and others attempting to learn more about our history and culture.)

THINK SPECIALIZATION. Here we have a wide variety of professions that often attract those who enjoy research and, at the same time, seek recognition. Many who are interested in this area eventually become teachers.

Specific Careers → 1.
2.
3.
4.
5.
6.
7.
8.
9.
10.

WILL THIS OCCUPATIONAL AREA;

	Yes	**No**
Measurably help you reach your life goals?	☐	☐
Be compatible with your values?	☐	☐
Capitalize on your special interests?	☐	☐
Challenge your mental abilities?	☐	☐
Take advantage of any aptitudes you were able to identify?	☐	☐
Make use of any special talents you may possess?	☐	☐
Provide the working environment you want?	☐	☐

Career Box #10

FARMING, FORESTRY, FISHING

(Includes all forms of land cultivation, animal production, mining, and food storage and transportation.)

THINK OUTDOORS. Most people in these careers prefer to be away from crowds. They enjoy being close to nature, are not afraid of hard work, prefer not to be restricted to regular hours, and might opt for a pickup truck rather than an automobile for family use.

Specific Careers → 1.

2.

3.

4.

5.

6.

7.

8.

9.

10.

WILL THIS OCCUPATIONAL AREA;

	Yes	No
Measurably help you reach your life goals?	☐	☐
Be compatible with your values?	☐	☐
Capitalize on your special interests?	☐	☐
Challenge your mental abilities?	☐	☐
Take advantage of any aptitudes you were able to identify?	☐	☐
Make use of any special talents you may possess?	☐	☐
Provide the working environment you want?	☐	☐

Career Box #11

MILITARY
(All careers found in the Army, Navy, Air Force, Marines, and Coast Guard.)

THINK PATRIOTISM AND DISCIPLINE. Many occupations exist in the field (support services range from office occupations to high technology), it is normally the most structured of environments. Many enjoy the status of a uniform.

Specific Careers → 1.
2.
3.
4.
5.
6.
7.
8.
9.
10.

WILL THIS OCCUPATIONAL AREA;

	Yes	No
Measurably help you reach your life goals?	☐	☐
Be compatible with your values?	☐	☐
Capitalize on your special interests?	☐	☐
Challenge your mental abilities?	☐	☐
Take advantage of any aptitudes you were able to identify?	☐	☐
Make use of any special talents you may possess?	☐	☐
Provide the working environment you want?	☐	☐

Career Box #12

HOSPITALITY

(Restaurant, hotel, travel occupations, etc.)

THINK SERVICE AND FRIENDLINESS. When you consider all of the eating places, hotels, resorts, amusement parks and recreational areas you soon realize that hospitality (serving others) is big business and getting bigger. Most who work in this area are people-oriented, willing to work odd hours, and like the lively, sometimes glamorous, atmosphere. Many who start out in a hospitality industry wind up in management positions or ownership roles.

Specific Careers → 1.

2.

3.

4.

5.

6.

7.

8.

9.

10.

WILL THIS OCCUPATIONAL AREA;

	Yes	No
Measurably help you reach your life goals?	☐	☐
Be compatible with your values?	☐	☐
Capitalize on your special interests?	☐	☐
Challenge your mental abilities?	☐	☐
Take advantage of any aptitudes you were able to identify?	☐	☐
Make use of any special talents you may possess?	☐	☐
Provide the working environment you want?	☐	☐

Career Box #13

ENTREPRENEURSHIP

(Owning your own manufacturing, wholesale, or retail business; becoming a franchisee. Operating a special service out of your home.)

THINK FREEDOM: Not everyone is geared to work for another individual or firm. To satisfy their values, some need to operate alone, even though they work harder and more hours than if they were on a payroll. Almost all of the career boxes listed (15) provide learning experiences that can lead to entrepreneurship.

Specific Careers → 1.

2.

3.

4.

5.

6.

7.

8.

9.

10.

WILL THIS OCCUPATIONAL AREA;

	Yes	No
Measurably help you reach your life goals?	☐	☐
Be compatible with your values?	☐	☐
Capitalize on your special interests?	☐	☐
Challenge your mental abilities?	☐	☐
Take advantage of any aptitudes you were able to identify?	☐	☐
Make use of any special talents you may possess?	☐	☐
Provide the working environment you want?	☐	☐

Career Box #14

UNUSUAL, EXOTIC OCCUPATIONS

(This category includes everything from being a curator in a museum, a singing messenger, to a dance therapist).

THINK DIFFERENT. Nobody can keep up with new careers that spring up daily in our society. Some people create their own jobs by doing something others have not thought of doing such as selling "pet rocks". If the career or job you have in mind does not fit into any of the other categories—and it has an unusual twist to it—consider this career box.

Specific Careers →

1.
2.
3.
4.
5.
6.
7.
8.
9.
10.

WILL THIS OCCUPATIONAL AREA;

	Yes	No
Measurably help you reach your life goals?	☐	☐
Be compatible with your values?	☐	☐
Capitalize on your special interests?	☐	☐
Challenge your mental abilities?	☐	☐
Take advantage of any aptitudes you were able to identify?	☐	☐
Make use of any special talents you may possess?	☐	☐
Provide the working environment you want?	☐	☐

Career Box #15

MISCELLANEOUS

WHEN A CAREER DOESN'T FIT EASILY OR COMFORTABLY INTO THE FIRST FOURTEEN BOXES, PLACE IT IN THIS ONE. This does not mean that it is a less exciting or unimportant career, it simply means it did not fit into one of the contrived career boxes.

Specific Careers ⟶
1.
2.
3.
4.
5.
6.
7.
8.
9.
10.

WILL THIS OCCUPATIONAL AREA;

	Yes	No
Measurably help you reach your life goals?	☐	☐
Be compatible with your values?	☐	☐
Capitalize on your special interests?	☐	☐
Challenge your mental abilities?	☐	☐
Take advantage of any aptitudes you were able to identify?	☐	☐
Make use of any special talents you may possess?	☐	☐
Provide the working environment you want?	☐	☐

BE SURE YOU ANSWER THE QUESTIONS BENEATH ANY CAREER BOX IN WHICH YOU ENTER A SPECIFIC CAREER POSSIBILITY. THEY WILL HELP YOU DETERMINE WHETHER THAT CAREER CLUSTER IS COMPATIBLE WITH YOUR GOALS, VALUES, INTERESTS, ABILITIES, APTITUDES, TALENTS AND VIEWS ABOUT A WORKING ENVIRONMENT.

SELECTING THE RIGHT CAREER BOX

You may have already decided on the career box that you think is best. The system (assigning specific careers to one of fifteen boxes) often explains itself and further explanation seems redundant. There are, however, a few cautions one might be wise to honor.

ANY CAREER BOX WITH A SPECIFIC CAREER LISTED IS DESERVING OF CONSIDERATION. Sometimes an individual is locked into one or two specific careers and either one or both are the only ones of interest within their best career area.

> Rachel only listed two careers (Registered and Psychiatric Nurse) in the Health Services career box but listed six in the Office Occupations box. Even so, her interest, values and life goals were stronger in Health Services. As a result, she made the right decision when she attended nursing school.

THE CAREER BOX THAT ATTRACTED MOST OF YOUR SPECIFIC CAREER CHOICES SHOULD BE CHALLENGED. Just because one box may have the largest number of specific careers listed does not automatically make it the best choice.

> To his surprise, Josh wound up with seven specific careers in the High Tech/Engineering box. Because of this he was tempted to make a selection out of the seven. However, in discussing his results with a guidance counselor, Josh recognized that his interest in becoming a biologist (Science box) was greater than he thought. The choice was also a better fit as far as his work environment preferences and other factors. His second and third choice, however, came from the High Tech/Engineering box.

SELECTING THE RIGHT CAREER BOX (Continued)

IT IS A GOOD IDEA TO REVIEW AND COMPARE "YES" AND "NO" ANSWERS IN ALL BOXES WHERE A CAREER WAS LISTED. It is possible that you may wish to do additional research in one career area (box) and want to rethink the potential it may have.

> Brad took time to answer all of the questions at the bottom of each box and discovered that he got more yes answers from the box 13 (Entrepreneurial) than others. This caused him to go back and spend more time on his list of twenty specific careers, making a few revisions. In the end, Brad settled for the Entrepreneurial box and expanded the specific career possibilities.

When the time comes to select the right career box, it is always a good idea to talk things over with another and do some extra thinking.

WHAT IS A CAREER PATTERN?

A number of occupations might make up your career pattern. For example, in the illustration below, the individual started out as a carpenter and wound up being a builder. In other words, your career pattern is where your occupations eventually lead you.

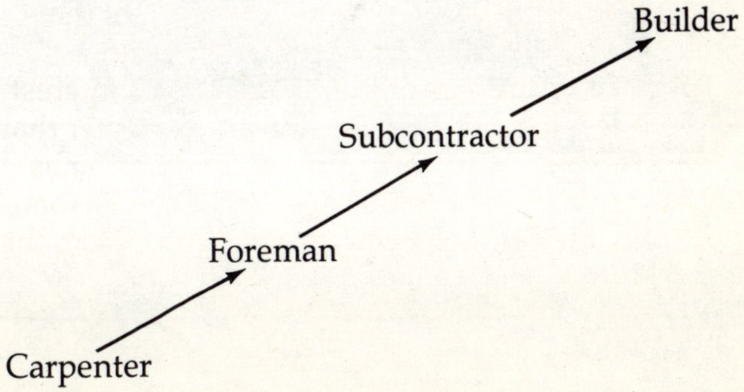

PART IV

SELECTING A SPECIFIC CAREER

ASKING YOURSELF QUESTIONS

Once you narrow down possible career choices you should learn as much about the career in question as possible. Far too many people commit themselves to a career without doing enough research. If these individuals would spend a few hours in a local library, campus career center, or best of all talking to others who have made a career choice in the same field, they could protect themselves against making a mistake they might regret later. Some career guidance specialists recommend that people do research at the initial point of selection (prospects) and further investigation after narrowing choices to three.

QUESTIONS YOU SHOULD BE ABLE TO ANSWER ABOUT ALL YOUR CAREER PROSPECTS

1. What are the specific training or educational requirements? What kind of training? How much education? Where are the schools located? What will it cost?
2. What other qualifications are needed? Does the career demand a certain trait, skill, or aptitude I do or do not have?
3. What is the nature of the work? Would I like it? Is it the sort of thing I could do over a long period of time?
4. What is the work environment? Is the occupation only in a factory? Office? Outdoors? Indoors? What about the hours?
5. What is the earning potential? Will I be able to make enough money to satisfy myself? Will I reach my salary peak too soon?
6. Where could I find such a job? Only in a big city? Would I like the geographical location?
7. What is the employment outlook? Good? Poor? Will there be openings after I complete my education?
8. Will the career permit me to live the life-style I seek? How much freedom will I have? What are the pressures? Will the job be at least somewhat in harmony with my personal values?
9. Does this career mean I would be forced to work for a big organization? If so, would I be able to cope with it?
10. Would I be successful? Would the career push me to live up to my potential? Or would I be underemployed in a few years?

#ONE RESOURCE BOOK

Locate an *Occupational Outlook Handbook* (OOH) published by the United States Department of Labor. The latest edition should be in any library or career center. It looks like a very large telephone book, and it is the best single source of up-to-date career information. It contains data on most occupations, including nature of work, educational requirements, earnings, conditions of work, and employment outlook. All of this information is vital to the decisions you will make later.

THE PROCESS OF ELIMINATION

The process of elimination is a sound procedure, especially when it comes to choosing a career. When you narrow your choices to a single career box, you have made excellent progress. When you can narrow your choice even further, the results are not only gratifying but probably reliable. Here are three suggestions to assist you in selecting a specific career from the career box you chose.

1. YOU MAY WISH TO DO SOME OUTSIDE RESEARCH TO LEARN MORE ABOUT THE SPECIFIC CAREERS IN YOUR CHOSEN BOX. You could, for example, go to a library or career center and read everything you can find about each career; or you could interview someone already occupying the career; or, if you are on campus, talk with a professor who teaches in the career area chosen.

> Jill had a good feeling about the career box she selected (General Business) but couldn't decide whether she wanted to be a CPA or take a more general course in Business Administration. After doing more reading and talking to her accounting professor she decided on becoming a CPA. Jill's excellent grades in accounting and her side interest in Data Processing helped her make the important decision.

2. ALTHOUGH THE QUESTIONS AT THE BOTTOM OF EACH CAREER BOX CAN BE HELPFUL IN DECIDING WHICH BOX IS BEST, THEY CAN BE OF EVEN MORE HELP IN SELECTING A SPECIFIC CAREER. It is recommended that the reader evaluate each specific career within a box based upon the questions. The one receiving the most yes answers should be given priority consideration.

> Doug was amazed to discover that twelve out of his twenty specific career choices fell into the Creative/Education/Religious box. As he went through the list (asking the seven questions) he discovered that the career of becoming a Journalist rated higher than others. Was he attracted to this career because he was a sports writer in high school? Did it combine all of the creative and educational aspects of other careers? At any rate, Doug decided on the basis of the answers to become a journalism major with a minor in education.

3. WHEN YOU ARE ON THE RIGHT TRACK YOU CAN DELAY SPECIFIC CAREER CHOICES UNTIL LATER. It is estimated by experts that 50% of those who graduate from college are, by their own admission, in the wrong major. This is a signal that they were on the wrong track from the start.

> Because of her high mental ability level, unusual mechanical aptitude, and interest in mathematical theory, Angelica knew she had found the right career box, but also recognized that it would take more education and time before she could make a specific career choice. After discussing the matter with her counselor, Angelica decided to spend a full year investigating the possibilities. She figured she needed to know exactly where she was going before entering graduate school.

DECISION TIME*

If you have conscientiously followed the system presented in the previous pages, you have reached a point where you should be able to make a tentative specific career choice. You may wish further verification in the future, but for planning purposes you can commit yourself now. In doing this, you are not closing the door on other options. Please write your choice below.

MY CAREER CHOICE AT THIS TIME IS:

____

CASE #4

(See next page)

*If you feel you need additional time to learn more about your leading career possibilities before making a decision, you should delay your decision until such research has been accomplished.

CASE #4

People often experience personal growth and leave unsatisfactory careers behind.

Also dynamic changes in the world of work can make careers obsolete.

That is why you may decide to review the process presented in this program at regular intervals.

MID-LIFE CAREER CHANGE

Richard is happily married with two teen-age children. For the last four years he has felt trapped in his position with a large corporation. There are three primary reasons Richard feels this way. First, the company is not experiencing the growth it experienced in the past. This limits opportunities for promotion. Second, Richard has a negative attitude about his immediate boss; and he knows top management is aware of his feelings. Third, Richard never made a career search and feels his talents have never been fully exploited.

With the help of an understanding wife, Richard has taken a close look at his values. He decided the following were most important.

1. A desire to be an entrepreneur—free from corporate politics.
2. An aspiration to stay in the same geographical area, with the same friends—probably in the same house.
3. A job where he can work with people—especially customers.

After devoting six months to a personal search, Richard has come up with three possibilities. ALL IN THE HOSPITALITY FIELD.

Start a travel agency.
Become a restaurant franchisee.
Manage a motel as a part owner.

How could Richard and his wife verify, ahead of time, they are making the right decision? Write your specific suggestion below.

____

____

____

Compare your opinion with that of the author on page 73.

PART V

VERIFICATION OF CHOICE

SATISFY YOURSELF

It is often difficult to be true to yourself especially when dealing with long term decisions such as your future. So, naturally, the selection of a career that is in harmony with your life goals is a heavy decision. This is why you may wish to take the following suggestions seriously.

Suggestion 1: TALK THINGS OVER WITH OTHERS. All career choices are, in a sense, tentative. You should discuss how you are feeling about possible careers with those close to you so they can either reinforce your feelings or, in some cases, raise questions and concerns.

Suggestion 2: CONDUCT SOME CAREER INTERVIEWS: There is no better way to verify what you have learned or what you anticipate than talking with someone who occupies the career position you are striving to reach. These individuals can usually be found in your own community and all it normally takes to set up an interview is a telephone call.

Suggestion 3: SPEND TIME IN THE APPROPRIATE WORK ENVIRONMENT: In some cases it is possible to get a part-time job or apprenticeship in a career area you wish to investigate. For example, if you were thinking about owning your own restaurant, you might become a waiter/waitress in one similar in size and menu to the one you envision owning. If you were thinking about becoming a nurse, you might work as a volunteer in a hospital or nursing home. Nothing can take the place of actual exposure in advance of a decision.

Suggestion 4: TALK TO A GUIDANCE EXPERT: If you are lucky enough to have a university or community college nearby, go to the guidance or career center and make an appointment to discuss your situation with a counselor. Take the results of your preliminary career search data with you. Ask the person you contact for suggestions on how to verify your choice. Are there any testing instruments that might help? Is there a computer-based program available? What reading is recommended?

As you take advantage of any or all of the above suggestions please keep in mind that when you are true to yourself, your future will often take care of itself.

CASE #5

CASE #5

When some people realize how much impact a career choice will have on their lives, they panic and lose confidence in their choice. This is unfortunate because after a good search has been completed—and the individual has a satisfied feeling—that person should usually go with the decision. If necessary, a career change can be made after further personal growth is experienced.

SECOND THOUGHTS

Mrs. Henderson has conscentiously completed a career discovery program similar to the one in this book. She found it difficult to list enough career possibilities but was able to place three of her choices inside the HEALTH SERVICES box. Her final choice was that of a Psychiatric Nurse.

Now Mrs. Henderson has second thoughts. Looking back over her efforts it all seemed too easy. Did she give sufficient consideration to her values? Did she apply what she learned from the case studies to her own situation? Will she be able to handle the advanced academic training?

Are Mrs. Henderson's misgivings natural? Is it possible to discover the *right* career so easily and quickly? Should Mrs. Henderson consider her program as only a "starter" and conduct a more in-depth search, using available interest inventories, personality tests, computer data base information, and other materials?

Would taking this program a second time in a few days or a few weeks give Mrs. Henderson more confidence in the system and her decision to become a Psychiatric Nurse?

Please write your answers in the space provided below and compare your answers with those of the author on page 73.

____

____

____

____

____

SHOULD YOU CONSIDER A DEEPER SEARCH?

Now that you have completed this short program, should you consider a more extended approach? Should you investigate a regular on-campus career guidance course? The list below is designed to help you make this decision. Please place a check in any square that applies to you.

- ☐ Taking the short-form program has made me interested in joining a group program (regular class) under the close guidance of a career expert. I feel that the results will be worth the extra investment in time.
- ☐ I appreciate the career choices from the short-form approach, but the results are not as convincing as I had hoped they might be. I think I need to do a full-fledged search before I will feel secure in my choice.
- ☐ I really skipped over the short-form program and, as a result, the results may not be as valid as they should be. I need to make a second effort and take it more seriously.
- ☐ I want more diagnostic assistance. I would like to take a few tests and have them interpreted to help me in my search.
- ☐ I need to make my search under conditions where I am under less pressure. In a few weeks, the timing will be better.
- ☐ I need constant support from both a teacher and other students if I am going to make a productive career search.
- ☐ I have yet to make a firm choice as to my college major and I want a more thorough search to make absolutely certain I am on the right educational track.
- ☐ The reason I want to become involved in a deeper career search is so I can get to know myself better. Finding the right career is secondary to me.
- ☐ I need more time to focus on a life goal.

FOLLOW-UP CHECK LIST

Place a mark in the square opposite those action steps you intend to take within the next few weeks.

- ☐ Discuss the life goal (or goals) I selected on page 12 with a close friend.
- ☐ Discuss the career choice I made on page 64 with the same friend, another individual, or a family member whose opinion I respect.
- ☐ Make an appointment with a career counselor to discuss the progress I have made.
- ☐ If my career selection requires additional formal education, make an appointment with an academic counselor to plan my future educational program.
- ☐ Discuss my career choice with someone already in the profession or job area.
- ☐ For validation purposes, wait two weeks and complete this program a second time.
- ☐ Go on a job-hunting expedition to find an interim position closer to my career choice.
- ☐ Do some new financial planning (investigating scholarships, borrowing money, working during the summer etc.) to help me reach my new career goal.

TEST YOURSELF

Demonstrate you understand the value of a career search by answering the following true and false questions. Correct answers will be found at the bottom of the page.

True	False	
______	______	1. When tied to life goals, a career search is easier *and* more valid.
______	______	2. There is little relationship between a career and personal identity search.
______	______	3. Career goals can become life goals.
______	______	4. A short career search using a good system will normally produce results equal to a more indepth search.
______	______	5. Talents and aptitudes are more similar than interests and abilities.
______	______	6. A person considering college needs to do a career search so that she or he can get on the best academic track.
______	______	7. Clustering specific career possibilities (chosen in advance) is a good way to verify whether one is heading in the right general direction.
______	______	8. Most colleges do not employ professional career specialists.
______	______	9. When you tie a career search to a life goal you are being true to your future.
______	______	10. By completing this program you have, in effect, started to write your own career script.

ANSWERS: 1. T 2. F 3. T 4. F 5. T 6. T 7. T 8. F 9. T 10. T

AUTHOR'S SUGGESTED ANSWERS TO CASES

A Problem For Joyce. Joyce has a classic career-lifestyle conflict. If she pursues her career as an executive, it will be difficult to enjoy the lifestyle she seems to want. On the other hand, she may have to accept a career that is not her first choice to live in the environment she prefers. Countless people face this same problem every day. The author believes Joyce can reach her goal as an executive and still pretty much lead the lifestyle she wishes. It will probably not happen in the beginning; but once Joyce has enjoyed some success, she can live in a rural-life setting and commute.

Jake's Dilemma. Even with Jake's determination and a strong tutor, it is doubtful whether or not he would earn an engineering degree. Jake must understand the difference between theoretical engineers and practical engineers. Jake falls in the latter classification. Here, he could be successful and probably would be happier. It would probably be better for Jake to take a demanding two-year technical program, than place himself under the pressure required in going after an engineering degree. There is a danger that Jake may become so discouraged he will throw in the educational towel and injure his future.

Will Joe Find The Right Career? If Joe sticks with his plan, he probably will do fine. It would be best, however, if Joe invested time in a "Career Search" class (with or without credit) so his search process would be more structured. Also, he would gain appropriate reinforcement from his teacher and fellow students. Most people who initiate a career-finding program never fully complete it. Joe is to be congratulated for trying to select a career on his own. It is estimated that only a small percentage of those in college make any serious attempt to systematically select a career.

Mid-Life Career Change. Once Richard leaves his current job, a good way to select which entrepreneurial path to follow is to continue living where they are and find a way to work part-time in each of the prospective work environments. Whenever it is possible to test out a career environment by becoming a part of it, a better decision can usually be made.

Second Thoughts. When it comes to a career choice, second thoughts are natural and should be expected. If Mrs. Henderson did a conscientious job, her misgivings may not be justified; and she should have confidence in CAREER DISCOVERY as well as in her own decision-making ability.

Mrs. Henderson should be encouraged to do a more in-depth search if she has the time. Such a search may eliminate some of her misgivings. It is possible she could come up with a choice different from that of Psychiatric Nurse.

Mrs. Henderson should, also, be encouraged to complete CAREER DISCOVERY a second time. It is vital she be totally committed to her choice before she begins the difficult educational workload necessary to reach her goal.

NOTES

NOTES

NOTES

NOTES

NOTES

NOTES

NOTES

TITLES IN THE VIVA-CRISP 50 MINUTE SERIES

ISBN	Title / Author	Price Rs. 99/- Each
SUPERVISORY SKILLS		
— 8176495042	**Accountability** by Sam R. Lloyd	
— 8176495239	**Building Trust** by Mary Shurtleff	
— 8176495654	**Excellence in Supervision** by Rick Conlow	
— 8176495700	**From Technical Specialist to Supervisor** by Donald Shandler	
— 8176497150	**Supervising for Success** by Tony Moglia	
— 8176497223	**The New Supervisor** by Elwood N. Chapman	
TEAM BUILDING AND LEADERSHIP		
— 8176495069	**Achieving Consensus** by Jon Scott & Eileen Flanigan	
— 8176495662	**Facilitation Skills for Team Leaders** by C. Martin & D. Hackett	
— 8176495824	**Leadership Skills for Women** by M. Manning & P. Haddock	
— 8176495832	**Learning to Lead** by E. N. Chapman & P. Heim	
— 8176494542	**Motivating at Work** by Twyla Dell	
— 8176496782	**Team Building** by Robert B. Maddux	
— 8176497177	**Team Problem Solving** by Sandy Pokras	
— 8176497312	**Virtual Teaming** by D. Jude-York & L. Davis	
— 8176497347	**Working in Teams** by Sandy Pokras	
MANAGEMENT SKILLS		
— 8176495468	**Delegating For Results** by Robert B. Maddux	
— 8176495735	**Goals and Goal Setting** by Larrie A. Rouillard	
— 8176495778	**Improving Your Company Image** by Sylvia Blishak	
— 8176495948	**Managing the Technical Professional** by Herbert Kindler	
— 8176494550	**Multipoint Feedback** by D. Jude-York & S. Wise	
— 8176494577	**Project Management** by Marion E. Haynes	
— 8176497053	**Retaining Your Employees** by B. Wingfield & J. Berry	
— 8176497126	**Successful Negotiation** by Robert B. Maddux	
— 8176497215	**The Ecstatic Buzz of Doing Business** by J. Bado & C. Ivanacic	
— 8176495808	**The Internal Consultant** by Marcia Meislin	
INCREASE EMPLOYEE PERFORMANCE		
— 8176495530	**Downsizing Without Disaster** by Lynn Tylczak	
— 8176495573	**Effective Performance Appraisals** by Robert B. Maddux	
— 8176495638	**Empowerment** by C. Scott & D. Jaffe	
— 8176495743	**Handling the Difficult Employee** by Marty Brounstein	

ISBN	Title / Author	Price Rs. 99/- Each
— 8176495867	**Managing Anger** by Rebecca Luhn Wolfe	
— 8176495891	**Managing for Commitment** by Carol Kinsey Goman	
— 8176495905	**Managing Negative People** by S. Michael Kravitz	
— 8176496960	**Partners in Performance** by Tony Moglia	
	COACHING AND MENTORING	
— 8176495166	**Be Your Own Coach** by B. Braham & C. Wahl	
— 817649531X	**Coaching and Counseling** by Marianne Minor	
— 8176495328	**Coaching for Development** by Marianne Minor	
— 8176495859	**Making the Most of Being Mentored** by Gordon F. Shea	
— 8176495999	**Mentoring** by Gordon F. Shea	
	VERBAL COMMUNICATION	
— 8176496731	**50 One-Minute Tips to Better Communication** by P. E. Bozek	
— 8176495336	**Communicating With Employees** by Frank M. Corrado	
— 8176495557	**Effective Meeting Skills** by Marion E. Haynes	
— 8176495611	**Emotional Intelligence Works** by M. Kravitz & S. D. Schubert	
— 8176495727	**Giving and Receiving Feedback** by Patti Hathaway	
— 8176495840	**Making Humor Work** by Terry Paulson	
— 8176495107	**The Art of Communicating** by Bert Decker	
— 8176495255	**The Business of Listening** by Diana Bonet	
— 817649724X	**Thinking on Your Feet** by Marlene Caroselli	
	WRITTEN COMMUNICATION	
— 8176495190	**Better Business Writing** by Susan L. Brock	
— 8176495301	**Clear Writing** by Diana Bonet	
— 8176495670	**Fat-Free Writing** by Carol Andrus	
— 8176496928	**Powerful Proofreading Skills** by D. Smith & H. Sutton	
— 8176497193	**Technical Writing in the Corporate World** by H. Estrin & N. Elliot	
— 8176495220	**The Building Blocks of Business Writing** by Jack Swenson	
— 8176497371	**Writing Business Proposals and Reports** by Susan L. Brock	
— 8176497398	**Writing Fitness** by Jack Swenson	
— 8176497401	**Writing That Sells** by Kathleen A. Begley	
	PRESENTATION SKILLS	
— 8176495581	**Effective Presentation Skills** by Steve Mandel	
— 8176497185	**Technical Presentation Skills** by Steve Mandel	
— 8176497304	**Using Visual Aids** by C. Raines & L. Williamson	

ISBN	Title / Author	Price Rs. 99/- Each

ELECTRONIC COMMUNICATION

— 817649738X **Writing Effective E-Mail** by Nancy Flynn

CONFLICT RESOLUTION

— 8176495883 **Managing Disagreement Constructively** by Herbert S. Kindler

CUSTOMER SERVICE

— 8176496839 **A Positive Guide to Superior Service** by William Martin

— 8176495018 **Beyond Customer Service** by Richard F. Gerson

— 8176496863 **Calming Upset Customers** by Rebecca Morgan

— 8176495441 **Customer Satisfaction** by Dru Scott

— 8176495921 **Managing Quality Customer Service** by William B. Martin

— 8176495972 **Measuring Customer Satisfaction** by R. Gerson

— 817649691X **Most Customer Services Start With the Telephone** by Nancy Friedman

TELEPHONE SKILLS

— 8176497207 **Telephone Courtesy & Customer Service** by Lloyd C. Finch

CALL CENTER SUCCESS

— 8176495271 **Call Center Success** by Lloyd C. Finch

SALES AND MARKETING

— 8176496847 **Achieve Large-Budget Marketing Without a Large Budget** by Richard Gerson

— 8176495204 **Building and Closing the Sale** by V. Thornton

— 8176495263 **Business Research** by P. Timm & R. Farr

— 8176495360 **Consultative Sales Power** by Karen Mantyla

— 817649545X **Dealing Effectively With the Media** by John Wade

— 8176495514 **Direct Marketing Techniques** by Lois Geller

— 8176495603 **Effective Sales Management** by Tom Johnson

— 8176495964 **Marketing Your Consulting or Professional Services** by D. Karlson

— 8176497029 **Prospecting: The Key to Sales Success** by Virden Thornton

— 8176496774 **Sales Training Basics** by Elwood Chapman

— 8176497339 **Winning the Inner Game of Selling** by Richard Gerson

PRODUCTIVITY

— 8176495085 **Achieving Results** by Lorna Riley

— 8176495093 **Administrative Assistant** by Brenda Bailey-Hughes

— 8176496820 **Plan Your Work: Work Your Plan** by James Sherman

— 8176497134 **Successful Self-Management** by Paul R. Timm

ISBN	Title / Author	Price Rs. 99/- Each
	TIME MANAGEMENT	
— 817649674X	**Office Management** by M. Manning & P. Haddock	
— 8176496766	**Personal Time Management** by Marion E. Haynes	
— 8176497010	**Professionalism in the Office** by Marilyn Manning	
— 8176497231	**The Telephone and Time Management** by Dru Scott	
	SELF IMPROVEMENT	
— 8176495077	**Achieving Job Satisfaction** by Editors of Crisp Publications, Inc	
— 8176495123	**Attitude** by E. Chapman & W. Mcknight	
— 8176495298	**Clear and Creative Thinking** by Herb Kindler	
— 8176495344	**Concentration** by Sam Horn	
— 8176495433	**Critical Thinking** by Daniel A. Feldman	
— 8176495492	**Developing Positive Assertiveness** by Sam R. Lloyd	
— 8176495506	**Developing Self-Esteem** by Connie Palladino	
— 8176495646	**Ethics in Business** by R. Maddux & D. Maddux	
— 817649688X	**Finding Your Purpose** by Barbara J. Braham	
— 8176495980	**Memory Skills in Business** by Madelyn Burley-Allen	
— 8176497061	**Risk Taking** by Herbert Kindler	
	JOBS AND CAREERS	
— 817649528X	**Career Discovery Program** by Elwood N. Chapman	
— 8176495409	**Creating Your Skills Portfolio** by Carrie Straub	
— 8176495565	**Effective Networking** by Venda Raye-Johnson	
— 8176495719	**Getting Hired** by Richard Pinsker	
— 8176494569	**Networking for Success** by Nancy Flynn	
— 8176496944	**Preparing for the Behavior-Based Interview** by T. Fitzwater	
— 8176497002	**Preparing for Your Interview** by Diane Berk	
— 8176497088	**Strategic Resumes** by Marci Mahoney	
— 817649741X	**Your First Thirty Days** by E. Chapman & R. Maddux	
	PEER RELATIONS & APPEARANCE	
— 8176495247	**Business Etiquette & Professionalism** by M. Kay duPont	
— 817649576X	**Improving Peer Relationships** by Norman Hill	
— 8176495786	**Influence** by Elaina Zuker	
— 8176495794	**Influencing Others** by William Nothstine	
— 8176495956	**Managing Upward** by Patti Hathaway	
— 8176496936	**Office Politics** by Rebecca Luhn Wolfe	

	ISBN	Title / Author	Price Rs. 99/- Each
—	8176495484	**Developing Instructional Design** by Geri McArdle	
—	8176495549	**Dynamics of Diversity** by Odette Pollar	
—	8176496898	**Graphics for Presenters** by Lynn Kearny	
—	8176497266	**Training Managers to Train** by David Hayes	
—	8176497274	**Training Methods That Work** by Lois Hart	
—	8176497355	**Working Together** by George Simons	
		STRATEGIC DEVELOPMENT	
—	8176496871	**Competency and the Learning Organization** by Donald Shandler	
—	8176495395	**Creating a Learning Organization** by Barbara Braham	
—	8176496758	**Organization Development** by Lenny Ralphs	
—	8176496952	**Organizational Vision, Values and Mission** by Scott, Jaffe & Tobe	
—	8176497142	**Successful Strategic Planning** by Stephen Haines	
—	8176497169	**Systematic Succession Planning** by Rebecca Wolfe	
—	8176494585	**Understanding Leadership Competencies** by Guggenheimer & Szulc	
		FINANCE	
—	8176495050	**The Accounting Cycle** by J. Jacquet & W. Miller	
—	8176495855	**Basics of Budgeting** by Terry Dickey	
—	8176495689	**Financial Analysis** by J. Gill & M. Chatton	
—	8176496987	**Personal Financial Fitness** by Allen Klosowski	
—	817649707X	**Starting Your New Business** by Charles Martin	
—	8176497290	**Understanding Financial Statements** by James Gill	
		CHANGE	
—	8176495387	**Coping With Workplace Change** by J. Jeffreys	
—	8176495875	**Managing Change at Work** by C. Scott & D. Jaffe	
—	8176495913	**Managing Personal Change** by C. Scott & Dennis Jaffe	
—	8176497282	**Understanding Organizational Change** by L. Fossum	
		MANUFACTURING AND INVENTORY	
—	817649514X	**Basics of Inventory Management** by J. Viale	
—	8176495158	**Basics of Manufacturing** by J. Viale	
—	8176495182	**Benchmarking Basics** by James Patterson	
—	8176495212	**Building a Total Quality Culture** by Joe Batten	
—	8176495816	**JIT Forecasting and Master Scheduling** by J. Viale	
—	8176495379	**The Continuously Improving Self** by J. Lickson	
—	8176497258	**TQM** by JoAnn Haberer & M. Webb	

Prices are subject to change without notice.